GREEN MACHINE

The Slightly Gross Truth about Turning Your
FOOD SCRAPS into **GREEN ENERGY**

illustrated by
REBECCA DONNELLY   **CHRISTOPHE JACQUES**

GODWINBOOKS

Henry Holt and Company
NEW YORK

Food grows and food goes
from the farm to the town,

to the market,
the kitchen, the plate.

WE MEET AND WE EAT.

When we're done, there's a mound
of the scraps left from all that we ate.

We pick out slick pits, crunchy husks, chewed-on cobs,

empty pods, stringy stalks, and bruised fruit.

They sit in the bin in a soft, soggy blob
till the truck picks them up on its route.

Call it Peels on Wheels or a truck full of yuck:

IT'S A FOOD SCRAPS COLLECTION MACHINE!

It takes all the waste
(and some slime and some muck)
to a place where the garbage goes green.

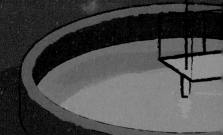

A place where the waste
isn't wasted: a tank
with the power to power our town,
where trash becomes gas,
and good riddance—that stank!

That's the power of food breaking down.

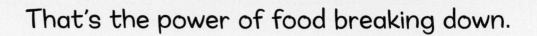

Inside this vast tank is a puddle of sludge—a wet mess.

GOOPY, SEWER-Y SOUP.

It's airtight in there, no O_2 for these bugs,
tiny microbes that eat food plus poop.

Machines grasp and glean
trash that's not the right type,
bits of plastic and metal and junk.

What's left is ground down
so it slides through the pipes
to combine with the rest of the gunk.

and some liquid
to mix them all in.

The bugs in the sludge do their slow, murky work.

ANAEROBIC DIGESTION BEGINS!

The goop stays for days
in the tank, in the dark,
while the biogas forms—bubble-blub.

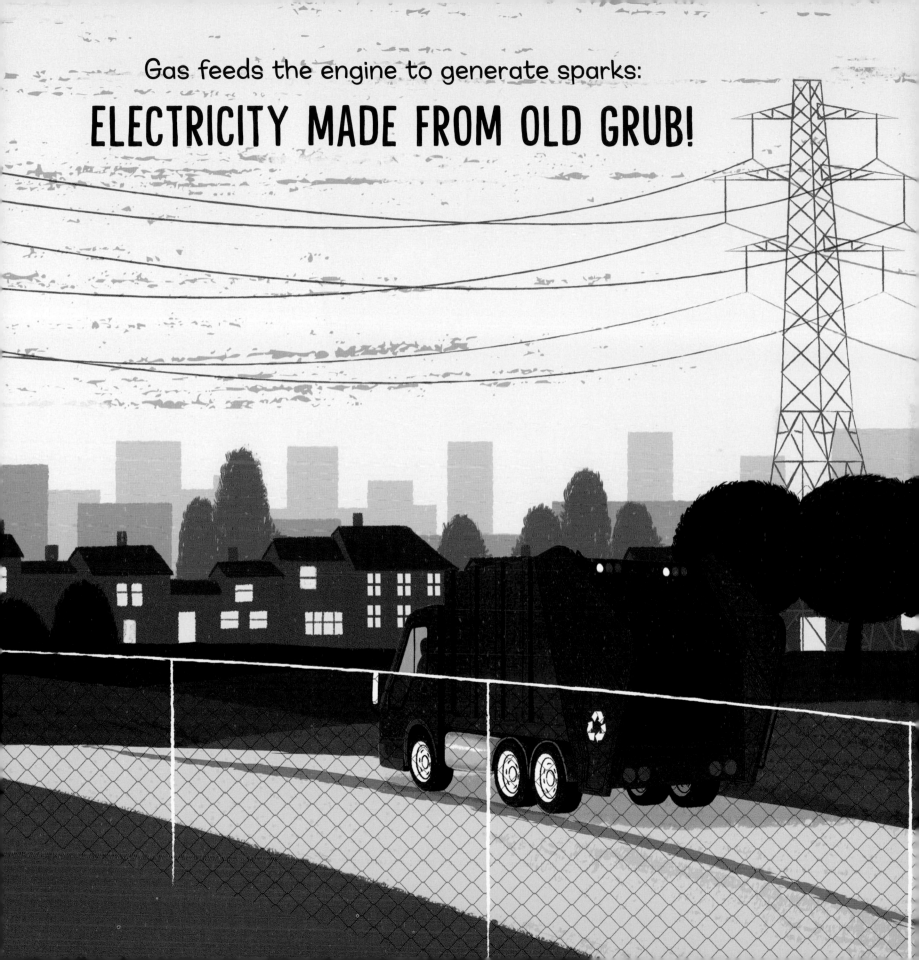

Gas feeds the engine to generate sparks:

ELECTRICITY MADE FROM OLD GRUB!

It flies through the wires
making light, making heat.

We gather in gathering dusk.
Celebration again!

We meet and we eat.
When we're finished, we gather the husks . . .

FOLLOW THE FOOD ENERGY!

Electricity is fed into the energy grid, available to light, heat, and power homes.

Composted food scraps are collected and transported to a processing plant.

Biogas is produced and captured in the tank.

The gas travels through a pipe from the tank to a generator, where it is processed to make electricity.

Food scraps are cleaned of garbage and ground up.

Mixed with liquid, the food scrap sludge goes into the anaerobic digester, where bugs get to work.

WHY DO WE NEED GREEN ENERGY?

We need energy for many things in our lives: lighting, heating, cooking, running our appliances and electronics, and lots more! We can get that energy from nonrenewable sources (such as coal and natural gas), which are limited and will eventually run out, or from renewable sources (such as wind, sun, water, and biogas), which are naturally replenished. By using renewable—or *green*—energy, we can make sure that there are plenty of resources now and in the future.

Biogas is a particularly useful energy source because it comes from food and farm waste, keeping the material out of our landfills. When food waste breaks down in a landfill, it releases methane, a gas that contributes to climate change. By capturing methane in an anaerobic digester, we can keep it out of the atmosphere and put it to work!

HOW ANAEROBIC DIGESTION WORKS

In anaerobic digestion, microbes in airless environments convert material from plants and animals into biogas, a mixture of methane and carbon dioxide. This process happens naturally in bogs, ocean and lake bottoms, landfills, even cows' digestive tracts! In a man-made digester, anaerobic digestion takes place in a sealed tank, where the microbes break down food, manure, and other organic matter. The microbes need a warm and oxygen-free environment to create the biogas, which is turned into energy. Biogas can be used just like natural gas, propane, or any other kind of fuel. It can be burned directly for heating and cooking, or it can burn in an engine that generates electricity.

TYPES OF ANAEROBIC DIGESTERS

FOOD WASTE
Food waste digesters make biogas using food scraps from restaurant kitchens, grocery stores, and other

places that handle food. These digesters often use the energy they make to operate, without producing enough energy for other uses. Their main job is to keep food waste out of landfills, although if they are large enough, they can produce extra biogas, too. You couldn't power your home from just the food waste your family makes, but when you start bringing together a whole community's food scraps, it adds up.

A digester that runs on food waste will produce more energy per pound of scraps than one that runs on farm waste or wastewater from towns. That's because food contains more energy than waste—about three times as much, according to one study. Think about it: Manure is basically food that has been digested once, through an animal's digestive system or your own. Some of its energy has already been used as fuel for your body!

FARM WASTE

Digesters at farms mainly process manure, although crops and food waste can be added to the mix. Farm digesters vary in size: The more cows or other animals a farm has, the larger the digester needs to be to handle all that manure. The leftover liquid from anaerobic digestion can be used to fertilize fields, and the solids can be used as animal bedding.

MUNICIPAL WASTE

When you run your faucets or flush your toilet, the water (along with everything else) goes into the sewer and then to a wastewater treatment plant. Many wastewater treatment plants use microbes to break down the wastewater solids (that's poop), but the biogas is often burned off, not harnessed as energy. Some cities are trying to figure out how to convert all that energy into electricity. Some municipal digesters even take food scraps! The digester in this book is based on this type.

FIND OUT MORE

Environmental Protection Agency. "Anaerobic Digestion (AD)." epa.gov/anaerobic-digestion.

Quest. "Power Up with Leftovers." KQED Science, Jan. 11, 2010. Audio, 6:01 mins. ww2.kqed.org/quest/2010/01/11/power-up-with-leftovers/.

Stuckey, Rachel. *Energy from Living Things: Biomass Energy.* New York: Crabtree, 2016.

To Susannah —R. D.

With thanks to Nick Hamilton-Honey and intern Brady Bruno at Cornell Cooperative
Extension of St. Lawrence County for giving me my first look at an anaerobic digester (and
answering many questions); to Dr. Stefan Grimberg of Clarkson University for showing me
the campus food scraps digester (and answering more questions); to John Hake at East Bay
Municipal Utility District for going over the utility's food scraps recycling process with me;
to Casey Lyall for being an early reader; to Molly Ker Hawn for being a power unto herself;
and to Julia Sooy and Laura Godwin for being the first to see the potential in garbage. —R. D.

Henry Holt and Company, *Publishers since 1866*
Henry Holt® is a registered trademark of Macmillan Publishing Group, LLC
120 Broadway, New York, NY 10271 · mackids.com

ISBN 978-1-250-30406-3
Library of Congress Control Number 2019941034

Our books may be purchased in bulk for promotional, educational, or business use. Please contact your local bookseller or the
Macmillan Corporate and Premium Sales Department at (800) 221-7945 ext. 5442 or by email at MacmillanSpecialMarkets@macmillan.com.

First edition, 2020 / Design by Carol Ly
Printed in China by RR Donnelley Asia Printing Solutions Ltd., Dongguan City, Guangdong Province

1 3 5 7 9 10 8 6 4 2